LIVING THINGS

Anna Claybourne

Illustrated by Chrissy Barnard

WAYLAND

www.waylandbooks.co.uk

First published in 2014 by Wayland

Text copyright © Wayland 2014
Illustrations © Wayland 2014

Wayland
338 Euston Road
London NW1 3BH

Wayland Australia
Level 17/207 Kent Street
Sydney, NSW 2000

Series editor: Victoria Brooker
Series designer: Lisa Peacock

A CIP catalogue record for this book is available
from the British Library.
Dewey number: 570-dc23

ISBN: 978 0 7502 8279 6
Ebook ISBN: 978 0 7502 8791 3

10 9 8 7 6 5 4 3 2 1

Printed in China

Wayland is a division of Hachette Children's Books,
an Hachette UK Company
www.hachette.co.uk

Contents

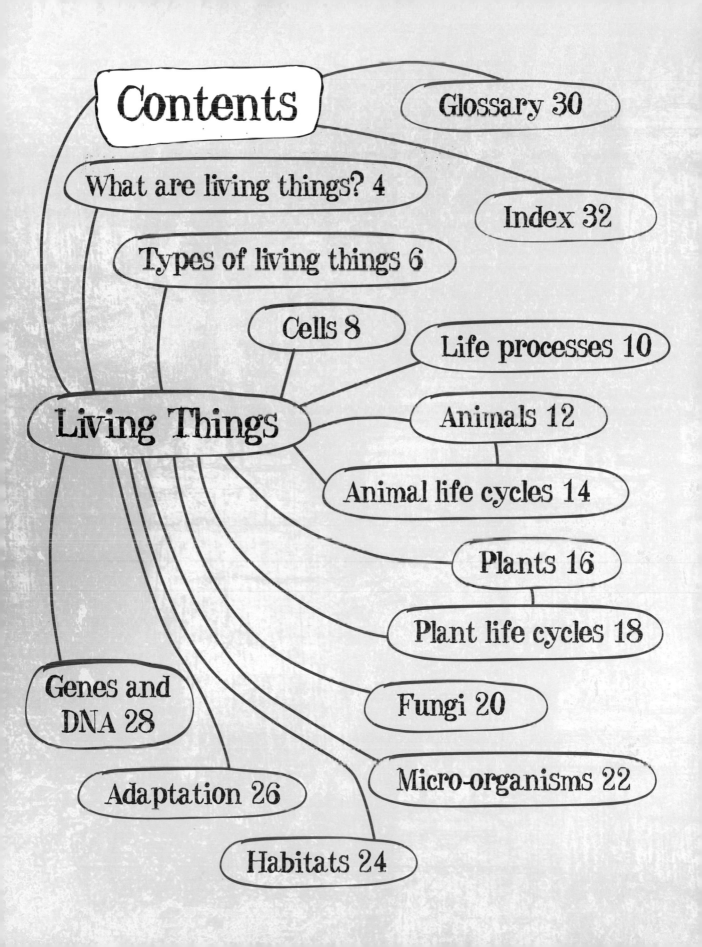

Glossary 30

What are living things? 4

Index 32

Types of living things 6

Cells 8

Life processes 10

Living Things

Animals 12

Animal life cycles 14

Plants 16

Plant life cycles 18

Genes and DNA 28

Fungi 20

Adaptation 26

Micro-organisms 22

Habitats 24

What are living things?

Our planet, the Earth, is the only planet we know of that is home to living things. Living things include plants, such as trees, grass and flowers, and animals, such as fish, frogs, birds, snakes, bees and elephants. Humans are a type of animal too.

There are also lots of fungi, including mushrooms and moulds, and micro-organisms – tiny living things too small for us to see. In fact, there are more micro-organisms than anything else. They include microscopic creatures living in seawater and in the soil, and tiny germs that cause diseases.

Species

Scientists have discovered and named around 1.5 million different types, or species, of living things. But there are many more still to be discovered. Scientists think there are probably more like 8 million species in total!

Each species can reproduce or have babies, making more living things like itself. In this way, a species can carry on existing through time. Living things have some other features in common too. As well as reproducing, they all move, grow, sense their surroundings, take in food, and turn food into energy they can use.

What is a mind web?

In this book, all the facts you need to know about living things are arranged into handy mind webs. A mind web is a way of laying out information about a topic on a single page. The topic title goes in the middle, with all the important facts and words arranged around it. There are lines to link things together, and little pictures to help you remember things.

Mind webs are great for helping you sort out, learn and remember facts and ideas. You can see a whole topic at a glance, and remind yourself all about it quickly and easily. Because the mind web looks like a picture, your brain may also find it easier to remember. Mind webs can also be called mind maps, spidergrams or spider graphs.

This mini mind web shows some of the main topics to do with living things.

Habitats

Animals

Cells

Living things

Plants

Fungi

athlete's foot

mould

spider

bee — octopus

toad

frog

invertebrates
(no backbone)

amphibians

mushrooms
and toadstools

yeast

Fungi

Animals

*Forficula
auricularia*
Common earwig

**Latin
names**

Types of living things

scientific name
for each species

Classification

**Micro-
organisms**

*Megaptera
novaeangliae*
Humpback whale

sorting living
things into
types

amoebas

protozoa

bacteria

E. coli

Panthera leo
Lion

malaria germ

salmonella

Panthera tigris
Tiger

Panthera pardus
Leopard

6

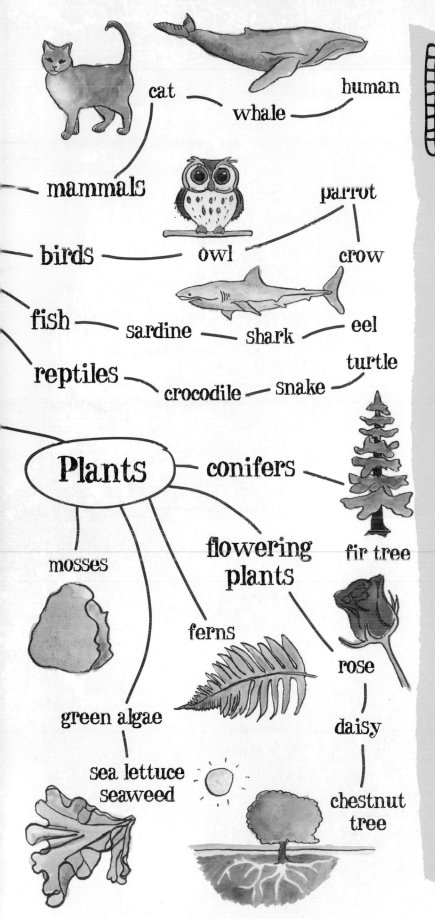

mammals — cat · whale · human

birds — owl · parrot · crow

fish — sardine · shark · eel

reptiles — crocodile · snake · turtle

Plants — conifers · fir tree

mosses

flowering plants · rose · daisy · chestnut tree

ferns

green algae

sea lettuce seaweed

Scientists sort out living things into groups. This is called 'classification'. There are various ways of classifying living things, but they usually have the same main groups. They are:

Animals: Animals feed on other living things. They can usually move around on their own and react quickly to things around them.

Plants: Plants use light energy, usually from the Sun, to help them make food. They are usually green, have roots and stay in one place.

Fungi: Fungi are like plants, but they do not use sunlight to grow.

Other living things: The remaining living things are mainly microscopically small creatures, or micro-organisms. This group includes bacteria and other tiny creatures like amoebas.

Latin names
Each species of living thing also has its own scientific name, written in Latin.

Cells

All living things are made up of tiny units called cells. Most cells are so small, you can see them only with a microscope. That means a large living thing like a human being, an elephant or a tree is made up of millions and millions of cells. However, there are also many kinds of much smaller living things with far fewer cells. There are a huge number of singled-celled creatures – living things made up of just one cell.

What's in a cell?

A cell is a tiny unit. It has its own skin, called the cell membrane, and tiny working parts called organelles. The organelles do different jobs inside the cell, just as the organs in your body, like your heart, stomach and lungs, do different jobs in your body.

Types of cells

Cells vary depending on the job they do. A human has about 200 different types, such as brain, muscle, skin and blood cells. Animal cells, plant cells and single-celled bacteria are different from each other too.

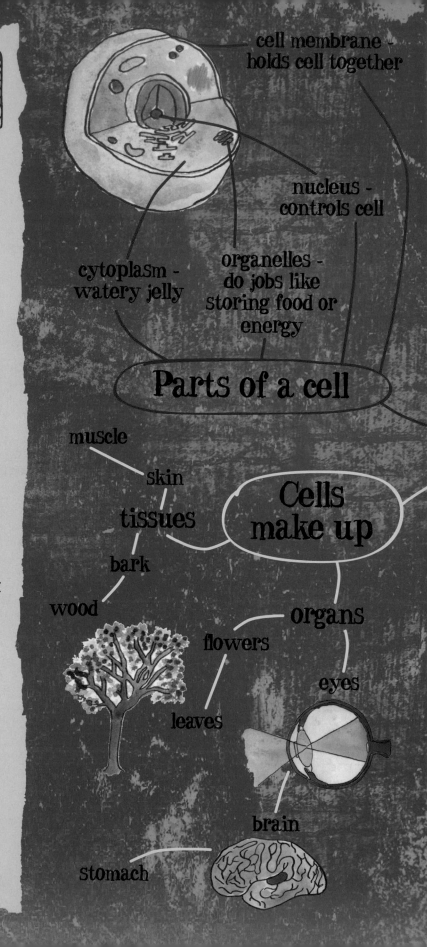

cell membrane - holds cell together

nucleus - controls cell

organelles - do jobs like storing food or energy

cytoplasm - watery jelly

Parts of a cell

muscle

skin

tissues

bark

wood

Cells make up

organs

flowers

eyes

leaves

brain

stomach

elephant - about 7,000 trillion cells

tiny worm - about 1,000 cells

human - about 10 trillion cells

Tiny units that make up living things

bacteria - 1 cell each

Cells

Bacterial cell

no separate nucleus

tail-shaped parts

organelles

cell wall

cell membrane

Animal cell

nucleus

Plant cell

cell membrane

large vacuole or space

thick cytoplasm

nucleus

cell membrane

organelles

organelles that collect sunlight

strong outer cell wall

9

run

crawl

swim

fly

animals

Movement

plants move towards light

Growth

animals -
babies grow
into adults

plants -
grow taller

Life processes

Excretion

Respiration

movement
energy

turning food into
energy

waste

animals

breakfast

plants
give out waste
gas

sweat

breathe out
waste gas

urine

10

having babies

animals

plants

making
seeds

Reproduction

dividing in
two

Single-celled
creatures

sense light

plants

sense gravity

Sensitivity

smelling

animals

seeing

hearing

HERE
BOY!

Nutrition

food

amoeba-
surrounds its food

plants -
use air, water
and light to
make food

animals -
eat other
living things

Life processes

There are some things that all living creatures do, known as the life processes. There are seven main life processes:

Movement: All living things move. A plant moves towards the light as it grows.

Reproduction: Living things have babies, or make more copies of themselves. Wolves have cubs, plants make seeds that become new plants, and bacteria make copies of themselves by dividing in two.

Sensitivity: Living things can sense their surroundings. A tree's roots sense gravity to help them grow downward.

Nutrition: All living things take in some kind of food to live on.

Excretion: All living things excrete, or give out waste.

Respiration: Respiration means turning food chemicals into energy.

Growth: All living things grow.

11

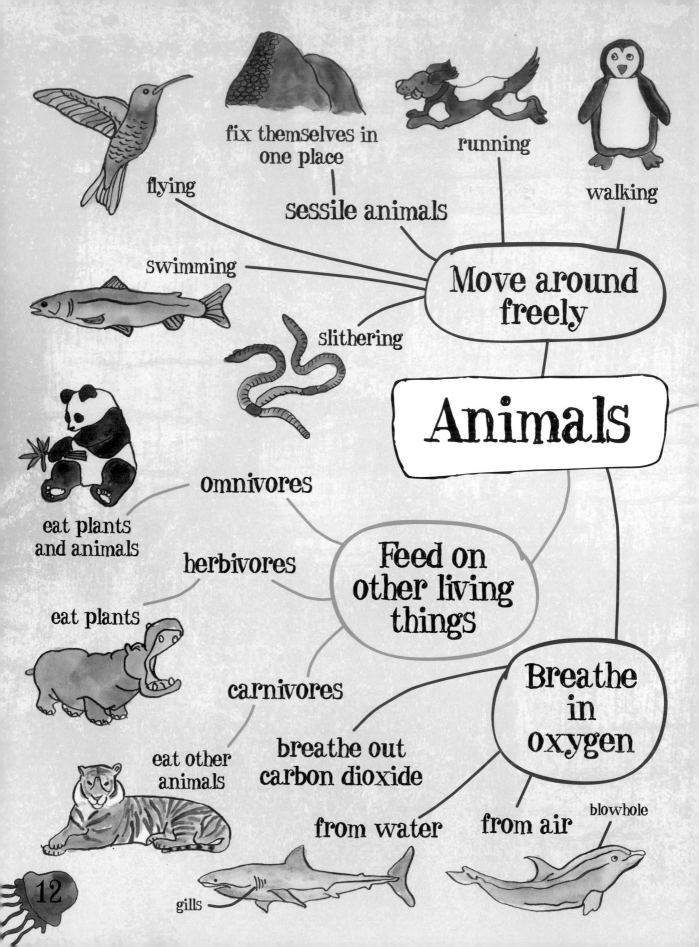

flying

fix themselves in
one place

running

walking

sessile animals

swimming

slithering

**Move around
freely**

Animals

omnivores

eat plants
and animals

herbivores

**Feed on
other living
things**

eat plants

carnivores

**Breathe
in
oxygen**

breathe out
carbon dioxide

eat other
animals

from water

from air

blowhole

gills

12

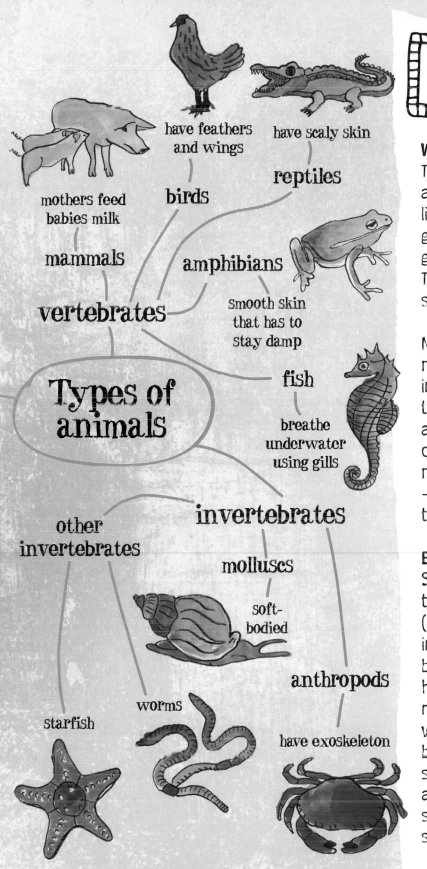

have feathers and wings

have scaly skin

reptiles

mothers feed babies milk

birds

mammals

amphibians

vertebrates

smooth skin that has to stay damp

Types of animals

fish

breathe underwater using gills

other invertebrates

invertebrates

molluscs

soft-bodied

anthropods

worms

starfish

have exoskeleton

Animals

What are animals?
The main features of animals are that they feed on other living things, breathe in oxygen gas, and breathe out another gas, carbon dioxide (CO_2). The word 'animal' means something that breathes.

Most animals also move around freely and independently – meaning they can move by themselves and go where they like. A few of them, however, spend most of their lives staying still – such as mussels, which fix themselves to rocks.

Backbones or no backbones?
Scientists divide animals into two main groups – vertebrates (animals with backbones) and invertebrates, which have no backbone. Vertebrates, like humans, cats and birds, have not just a backbone, but a whole skeleton inside their bodies. Invertebrates, like slugs, spiders and snails, have a soft body, sometimes with a shell or a protective hard outer skin, or exoskeleton.

caterpillar

cubs

male and
female cells

mothers feed
baby milk

female
lays eggs

pupa inside
cocoon

two
parents

tiger

male and
female cells

metamorphosis

Mammals

two parents

adult

moth

growth
of bud

bud
develops
mouth and
tentacles

Insects

hydra

bud breaks
off

Budding

Reptiles

whiptail lizard

turtle

one parent

babies fend for
themselves

two parents

eggs
hatch

gives birth
without mating

eggs

male and female
cells

14

frogspawn

tadpoles

male and female cells

froglets

two parents

frog

Amphibians

Animal life cycles

Animals reproduce, or have babies, in several different ways. Most animals make babies by combining two cells – one from a male and one from a female. When they join, they make a new cell that can grow into a baby.

In many other animals, the parents mate, and the male and female cells join inside the female's body. The female may then lay eggs, or grow the babies inside her body, then give birth to them.

One parent
Some animals need only one parent to reproduce. For example, some species of lizards are all female, and have babies without mating. The hydra, a simple sea animal, can have babies by 'budding' – a small part of the parent grows into a baby, then breaks off.

Birds

chicken

two parents

chicks

male and female cells

eggs

15

Plants

Plants are found all over our planet, and some are among the biggest of all living things. Unlike animals, most plants are rooted into the soil, and do not move around much. When they do, they move slowly. Plants can sense light and gravity, but they don't have eyes, ears or mouths.

Green machines

Inside their cells, plants contain a green chemical called chlorophyll. Chlorophyll allows plants to make food by combining water and carbon dioxide gas (CO_2) from the air, using energy from the Sun. This process is called photosynthesis, and it happens inside a plant's leaves. Plants are mainly green because of the chlorophyll they contain.

Flowers or no flowers?

Most of the plants around us are flowering plants — like fruit trees, buttercups, garden roses and daffodils. However, conifers have cones instead of flowers, and there are some non-flowering plants such as ferns and mosses.

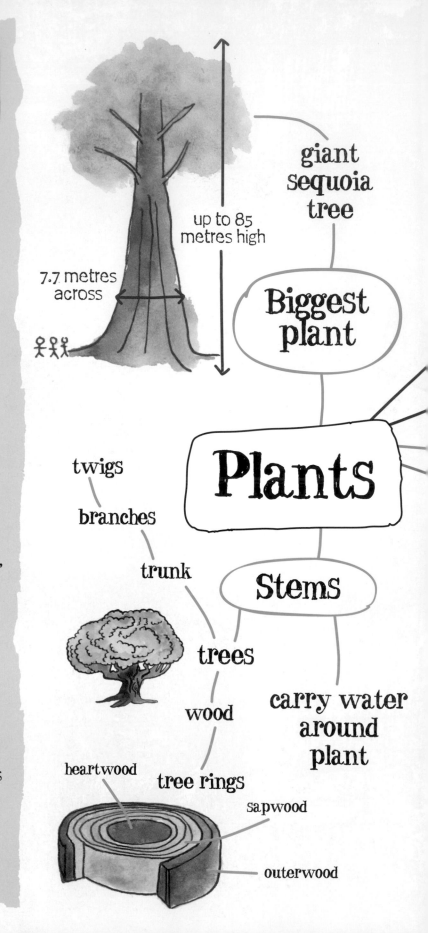

giant sequoia tree

up to 85 metres high

7.7 metres across

Biggest plant

Plants

twigs

branches

trunk

Stems

trees

wood

carry water around plant

heartwood

tree rings

sapwood

outerwood

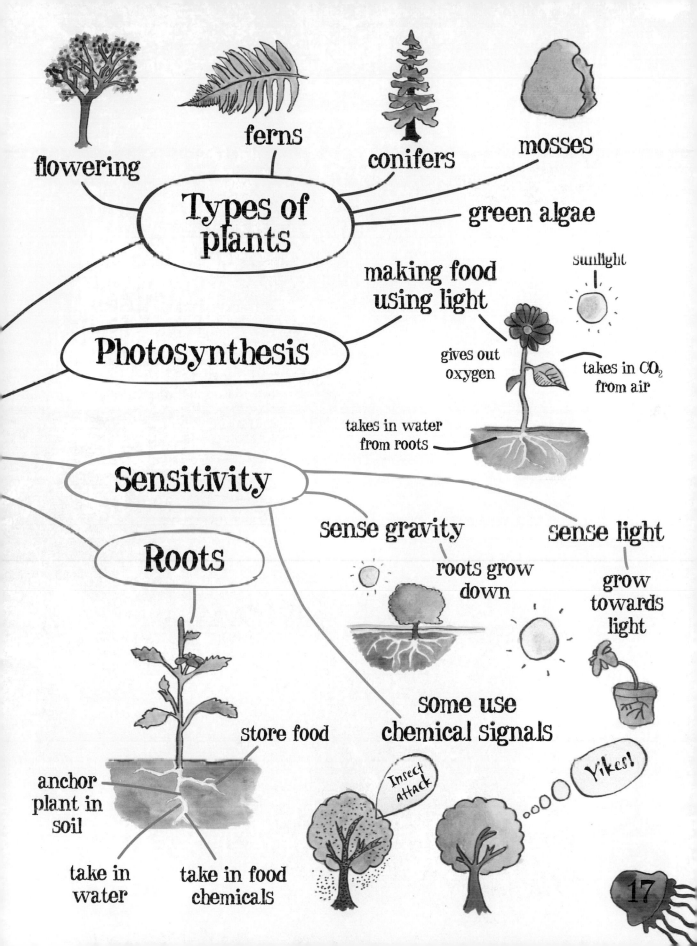

flowering

ferns

conifers

mosses

green algae

Types of plants

Photosynthesis

making food using light

sunlight

gives out oxygen

takes in CO₂ from air

takes in water from roots

Sensitivity

Roots

sense gravity

sense light

roots grow down

grow towards light

anchor plant in soil

store food

some use chemical signals

Insect attack

Yikes!

take in water

take in food chemicals

mosses

ferns

horsetails

apple tree

release tiny spores
instead of a seed

Seedless plants

strawberry

stalks spread
sideways

runners

Plant life cycles

Spreading out

rhizomes

Seed dispersal

roots spread
sideways

nettles

explodes to
shoot seeds

carried/
stored by
animals

in animal
droppings

squirting
cucumber

chestnuts

berries

18

pollen spread by insects

Stigma

apple flowers

pollen spread by wind or insects

ovary grows into fruit

seeds

Flowering plants

male cone

pollen

pine tree

female cone

Conifers

seeds form

female cells

wind

dandelion seeds

sycamore seeds

All plants reproduce and make baby plants like themselves. Like animals, they often do this by combining a male cell with a female cell. This makes a seed that can grow into a new plant. However, the male and female cells don't always come from different plants. Often they are both found on one plant.

Plants reproduce in other ways too. Some, like the dandelion, can make seeds without combining male and female cells. Others reach out sideways with special roots, called rhizomes, or stems, called runners. They grow into new plants that will separate from the parent plant.

Eat me!
Plant seeds often form inside sweet-tasting fruits like apples or cherries. Or the seed itself – like a chestnut – is delicious. Animals collect these, then drop them somewhere else, or eat them and spread the seeds around in their droppings. This helps the plant disperse its seeds far and wide.

cap

gills release spores that
grow into new fungi

stalk

mushroom

mycelium soaks up
food from soil

Fungi parts

help them rot away

fungal infection
feeds on dead skin
cells

**feed on dead
living things**

mould on
fruit

dead wood

**Fungi and
decay**

Fungi

dead insects

Fungi

Fungi are plant-like in some ways — they can grow in soil, and often have a network of thin, thread-like roots called the mycelium. But unlike plants, fungi are not green, and don't use sunlight to make food and grow. Instead, they feed on whatever they are growing on or in. Mushrooms often grow in soil or on old, dead wood. When you see mould growing on fruit or stale bread, that's a type of fungi too. Some fungi even grow on other living things, such as living plants, insects or even human skin.

How many cells?
Most types of fungi, like mushrooms and mould, have many cells. But one type, yeasts, are single-celled. They live together in big groups or colonies, so when you see fresh yeast, it looks a bit like a block of cheese. Yeast cells multiply, or increase in number, by budding. Each cell grows a new cell on its side, which gets bigger and bigger until it breaks off.

toadstools

puffball

fly agaric

bread mould

black mould

moulds

mushrooms

many-celled

yeast

athlete's foot

Single-celled

Types of fungi

parasitic fungi

cordyceps

two cells

Fungi life cycles

yeast

single cell

single cell

budding

Fungi as food

mushroom

spores

spore germination

edible mushrooms

yeast in bread dough

mycelium

food for animals

primordia

feeds

food for humans

flying squirrel

multiplies

makes gas bubbles

bread rises

not fully 'living'

even smaller than bacteria

tardigrades

nematodes

copepods

measles

chicken pox

flu

dust mites

tiny animals

tiny fungi

yeast

survive by invading cells

cause diseases

green algae

tiny plants

tuberculosis

sleeping sickness

malaria

Viruses

whooping cough

protozoa

Harmful micro-organisms

salmonella poisoning

bacteria

make yogurt

Helpful micro-organisms

protozoa

treat sewage

in plankton

help digest food

bacteria

yeast

make soil fertile

making beer and wine

make useful chemicals

making bread

provide food for sea creatures

22

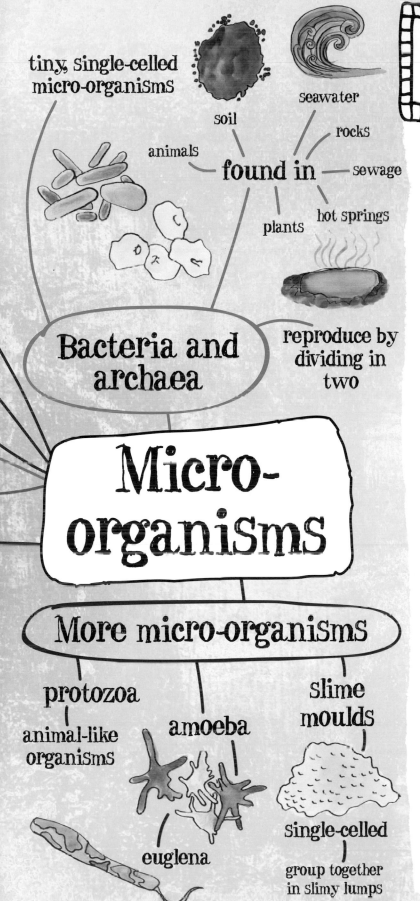

tiny, single-celled micro-organisms

seawater

rocks

soil

animals

sewage

found in

plants

hot springs

Bacteria and archaea

reproduce by dividing in two

Micro-organisms

More micro-organisms

protozoa

animal-like organisms

amoeba

euglena

slime moulds

single-celled

group together in slimy lumps

Micro-organisms are living things that are so small, we have to look at them with a microscope.

Types of micro-organisms

Scientists have discovered a **LOT** of different species of micro-organisms. Because they are so hard to see, there are probably many more still waiting to be found. Micro-organisms include the smallest members of the animal, plant and fungi families. They also include bacteria, and their relatives the archaea. These tiny creatures exist in huge numbers in all kinds of places — in soil, in water, deep in underground rocks, and inside larger living things, including humans. A large handful of soil contains more bacteria than there are human beings on Earth.

Helpful and harmful

Some micro-organisms are harmful to humans and can invade our bodies, causing diseases like tuberculosis and malaria. But others are helpful — for example, the bacteria living in our intestines help us to digest food.

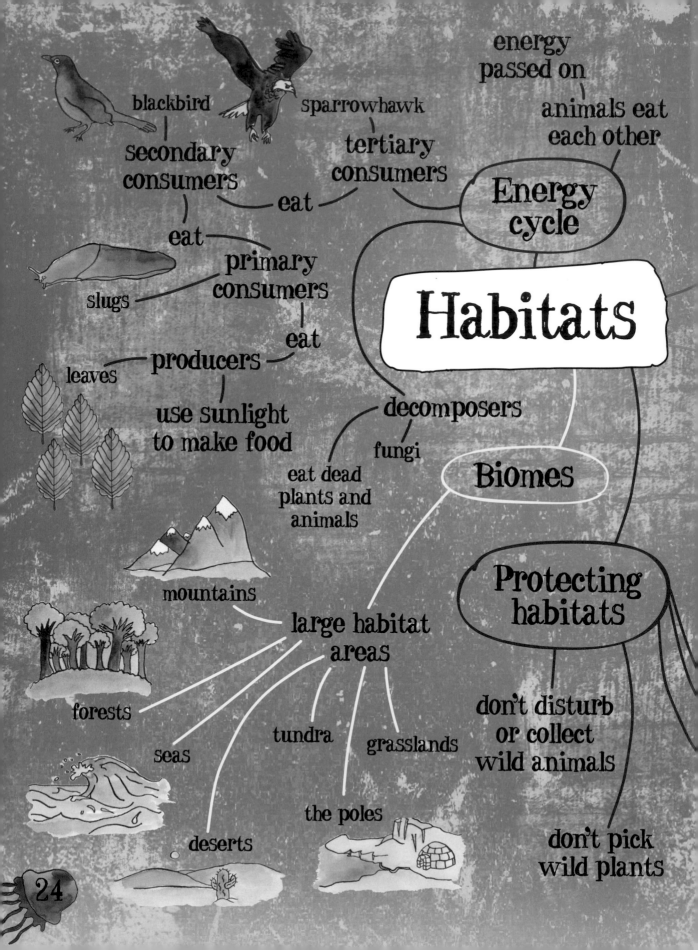

Habitats

Energy cycle
- energy passed on
- animals eat each other

Secondary consumers
- blackbird
- sparrowhawk — tertiary consumers

eat

eat

Primary consumers
- slugs

eat

Producers
- leaves
- use sunlight to make food

Decomposers
- fungi
- eat dead plants and animals

Biomes

Large habitat areas
- mountains
- forests
- seas
- deserts
- tundra
- the poles
- grasslands

Protecting habitats
- don't disturb or collect wild animals
- don't pick wild plants

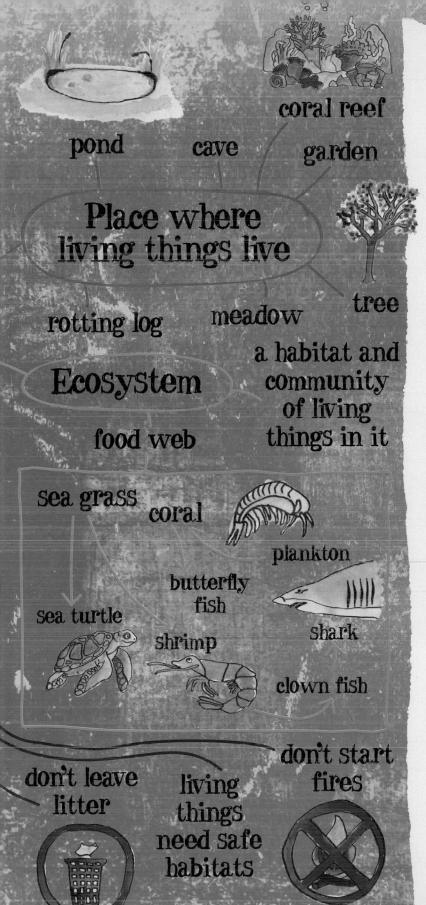

pond

cave

coral reef

garden

Place where living things live

tree

rotting log

meadow

a habitat and community of living things in it

Ecosystem

food web

sea grass

coral

plankton

butterfly fish

sea turtle

shrimp

shark

clown fish

don't leave litter

living things need safe habitats

don't start fires

Habitats

A habitat is the place where a species lives. All living things have their own habitats, where they can survive and find food. For example, a koala's habitat is a eucalyptus tree. Koalas are good at climbing and hanging onto branches, and they feed on eucalyptus leaves. If a koala didn't have this habitat to live in, it would be hard for it to survive.

Habitats can be quite small — a tree, pond, cave or garden could be a habitat. Biomes are larger areas that have a particular type of climate and surroundings — such as forests, deserts and mountain ranges.

Living together

Together, a habitat and the living things that live in it are called an ecosystem. In an ecosystem, each creature survives by feeding on something else that lives there. These relationships can be shown as food chains. A network of the food chains found in one ecosystem is called a food web.

25

Adaptation

Living things are amazingly well-suited to the places they live in. A whale, for example, has a streamlined shape for moving through water, thick blubber to keep it warm and a blowhole to help them breathe. All these features help it to survive in the ocean. But if you took a whale to live in the rainforest, it wouldn't last long!

Adapting to fit

Living things gradually adapt, or change over time, to suit their habitats. All species have variation. This means that they vary, or have slight differences from each other — even within the same species. In each habitat, the living things that survive best are the ones that suit that habitat best. They will find more food, escape from predators better and live longer. This means they are more likely to have babies and keep the species alive.

Living things pass on their features to their babies. So the features that suit the habitat best get passed on. Over time, species change, becoming adapted to their habitats. Another name for this is evolution.

26

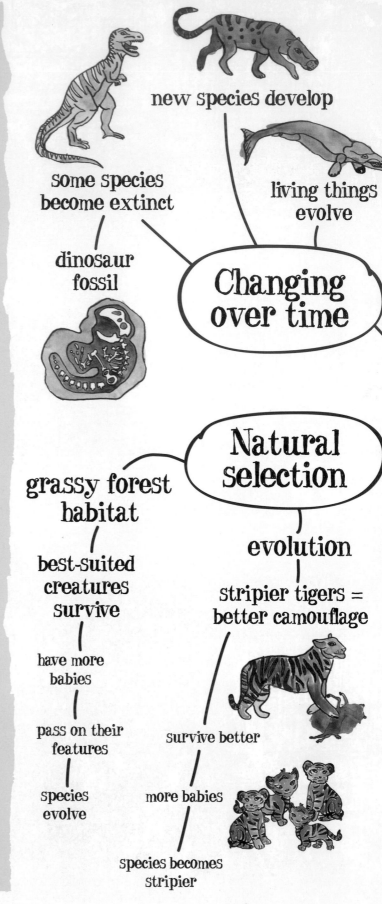

new species develop

some species become extinct

dinosaur fossil

living things evolve

Changing over time

Natural selection

grassy forest habitat

best-suited creatures survive

have more babies

pass on their features

species evolve

evolution

stripier tigers = better camouflage

survive better

more babies

species becomes stripier

blubber to keep warm

tail and fins for swimming

blowhole for breathing

killer whale

icy seas

tail that can grasp branches

hands for climbing

good eyesight for finding food

spider monkey

rainforest

rubbery hooves for gripping rock

warm woolly coat

good at jumping/ balancing

mountain goat

mountain peak

To habitat

Adaptation

floating leaf pads and flowers

pond

water lily

long stems so roots can reach mud

Variation

all species vary

each living thing is unique

tigers

all same species stripier

less stripy

Genes and DNA

gene contains instructions in a code that cells can read and understand. The instructions tell cells how to work and what to do.

All living things have DNA in their cells. DNA (short for DeoxyriboNucleic Acid) is a chemical that forms long, thin strings. They are found coiled up inside cells. Genes are sections of DNA. Each

Building a body

Each species has its own genome, or set of genes, which decide how it grows and what it looks like. For example, tigers' genes give them

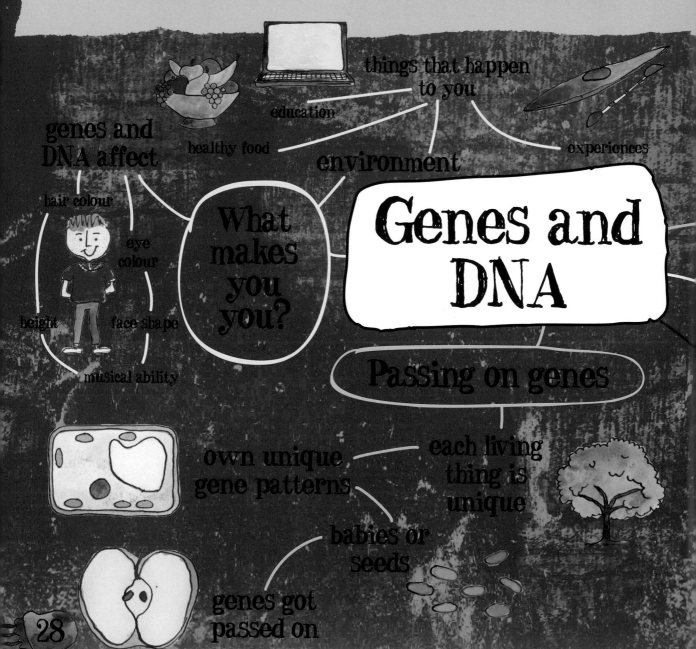

things that happen to you

education

genes and DNA affect

healthy food

experiences

environment

hair colour

eye colour

What makes you you?

Genes and DNA

height

face shape

musical ability

Passing on genes

own unique gene patterns

each living thing is unique

babies or seeds

genes got passed on

their big, strong bodies, stripy fur and sharp claws. Daisies have a different set of genes that make them grow roots, a stem and white flowers.

Genes also vary slightly within species. That's why daisies are slightly different from each other. So are people. Your genes make you a human, like other humans – but they also make you an individual, not quite like anyone else.

Passing it on

Whenever living things reproduce, they pass on copies of their genes to their babies. That's why tigers have baby tigers and daisy seeds grow into new daisies. It also explains why features like musical ability or red hair run in families.

mouse genome

apple tree genome

E. coli genome

mouse

apple tree

E. coli bacteria

human genome

Genome

set of genes for each species

human

DeoxyriboNucleic Acid (DNA)

Genes

section of DNA

cell nucleus

Genes tell cells

DNA

chromosome

how to reproduce

how to build body parts

how to grow

claws

stripes

Glossary

adaptation Changing to become more suited to the environment.

amoeba A type of single-celled living thing.

animal Living thing that breathes, moves around and eats other living things.

archaea A type of tiny single-celled living thing.

bacteria A type of tiny single-celled living thing.

biome Large area of a particular type of habitat.

blowhole Breathing hole on the head of a whale or dolphin.

blubber Thick layer of fat under the skin.

budding Way of reproducing in which the parent grows a baby from part of its body, which then breaks off.

carbon dioxide Gas found in the air, excreted by animals and taken in by plants.

cells Tiny units that make up all living things.

cell membrane Outer skin surrounding a cell.

chlorophyll Green chemical found in plant cells and used to collect sunlight.

classification The sorting of living things into groups and types.

DNA (DeoxyriboNucleic Acid) Spiral strand-shaped chemical that genes are made of.

disperse Spread out over a wide area.

ecosystem A habitat and the living things that are found in it.

evolution The way species change over time to become better at surviving.

excretion Giving out waste products, one of the life processes.

exoskeleton Hard outer skin or shell found on some invertebrates.

food chain Sequence of living things in which each one is food for the next.

food web Network of the various food chains that make up an ecosystem.

fungi Type of living thing that includes mushrooms, moulds and yeast.

genes Instructions found in cells that tell living things how to live and grow.

genome Set of genes belonging to a particular species.

habitat Place or surroundings where a living things live.

invertebrate Animal without a backbone.

larva Name for the young of some types of insects and other animals.

life processes Things that all living things do as part of being alive.

metamorphosis Changing shape or form as part of the life cycle of a living thing.

micro-organism Tiny living thing that is too small to be seen without a microscope.

mycelium Network of thread-like roots or hairs found in many fungi.

nucleus Control centre of a cell.

nutrition Another name for food and feeding, and one of the life processes.

organelles Tiny mini-organs found inside cells.

oxygen Gas found in the air, excreted by plants and taken in by animals.

photosynthesis Making food using carbon dioxide, water and sunlight.

plant Living thing that uses sunlight to make food and is usually rooted in one place.

predator Animal that hunts and eats other animals.

primordia An organ or part in the earliest stage of development.

reproduce To have babies or young.

respiration Converting food into useful energy, one of the life processes.

rhizome Plant root that grows sideways underground and gives rise to new plants.

runner Plant stem that grows sideways and roots into the soil to create new plants.

sensitivity Ability to sense and respond to surroundings, and one of the life processes.

single-celled Having only one cell.

species A particular type of living thing.

variation Slight differences between living things, including within the same species.

vertebrate Animal with a backbone.

yeast Type of single-celled fungus.

Index

adaptation 26–27, 30
amoebas 11, 23, 30
animals 6, 7, 8, 9, 10, 11, 12–15, 18, 19, 21, 22, 23, 24, 26, 27, 28, 29, 30
amphibians 6, 13, 14
archaea 23, 30

babies 10, 11, 13, 14–15, 26, 28, 29
bacteria 6, 7, 8, 9, 11, 22, 23, 29, 30
biomes 24, 25, 30
birds 7, 13, 15, 24
breathing 10, 12, 13, 26, 27
budding 15, 20, 21, 30

carbon dioxide 13, 12, 16, 17, 30
cells 8–9, 14, 15, 16, 19, 20, 21, 22, 28, 29, 30
chlorophyll 16, 30
classification 6, 7, 30

DNA 28–29, 30
dispersal 18, 19, 30

ecosystems 25, 30

evolution 26, 30
excretion 10, 11, 30

feeding 7, 11, 12, 13, 17, 20, 21, 22, 24, 25
fish 7, 13, 25
flowers 7, 16, 19
food webs 25, 30
fungi 6, 7, 20–21, 22, 23, 24, 30

genes 28–29, 30
growth 10, 11, 17, 19, 20, 28, 29

habitats 24–25, 26, 30
humans 4, 7, 8, 9, 13, 20, 21, 23, 29

insects 14, 17, 19, 20
invertebrates 6, 13, 30

mammals 7, 13, 14
metamorphosis 14, 31
micro-organisms 6, 7, 22–23, 31
moulds 6, 20, 21, 23
movement 10, 11, 12, 13
mushrooms 6, 20, 21

oxygen 12, 13, 17, 31

photosynthesis 16, 17, 31
plants 7, 8, 9, 10, 11, 12, 16–19, 20, 22, 23, 24, 31
reproduction 4, 11, 14–15, 18–19, 21, 23, 29, 31
reptiles 13, 15
respiration 10, 11, 31
rhizomes 18, 19, 31
roots 7, 11, 17, 19, 20, 27, 29
runners 18, 19, 31

seeds 11, 18, 19, 28, 29
sensitivity 11, 17, 31
single-celled things 8, 11, 20, 21, 23, 31
species 4, 6, 23, 25, 26, 27, 28, 29, 31
spores 18, 20, 21
sunlight 7, 9, 11, 16, 17, 24

variation 26, 27, 31
vertebrates 13, 31

water 11, 12, 16, 17, 23

yeasts 6, 20, 21, 22, 31